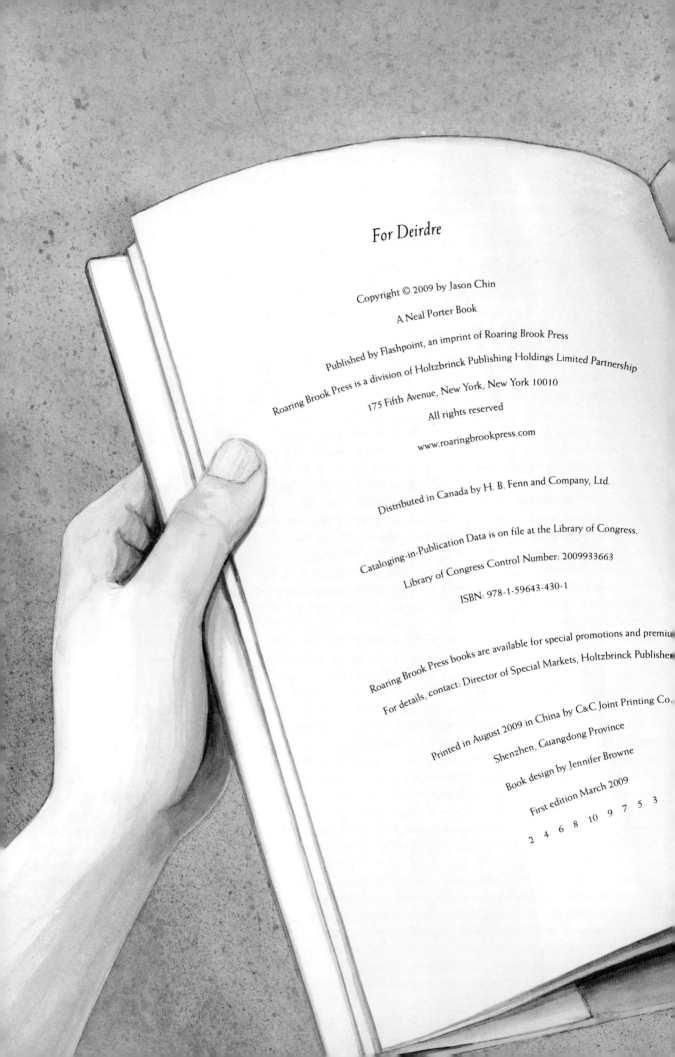

For Deirdre

Copyright © 2009 by Jason Chin

A Neal Porter Book

Published by Flashpoint, an imprint of Roaring Brook Press

Roaring Brook Press is a division of Holtzbrinck Publishing Holdings Limited Partnership

175 Fifth Avenue, New York, New York 10010

All rights reserved

www.roaringbrookpress.com

Distributed in Canada by H. B. Fenn and Company, Ltd.

Cataloging-in-Publication Data is on file at the Library of Congress.

Library of Congress Control Number: 2009933663

ISBN: 978-1-59643-430-1

Roaring Brook Press books are available for special promotions and premiu

For details, contact: Director of Special Markets, Holtzbrinck Publishe

Printed in August 2009 in China by C&C Joint Printing Co.

Shenzhen, Guangdong Province

Book design by Jennifer Browne

First edition March 2009

2 4 6 8 10 9 7 5 3

REDWOODS

JASON CHIN

Rb *Flash Point*

A NEAL PORTER BOOK
ROARING BROOK PRESS
NEW YORK

The coast redwoods are among
the oldest trees in the world.

Their ancestors lived about 165 million years ago, during the Jurassic period.

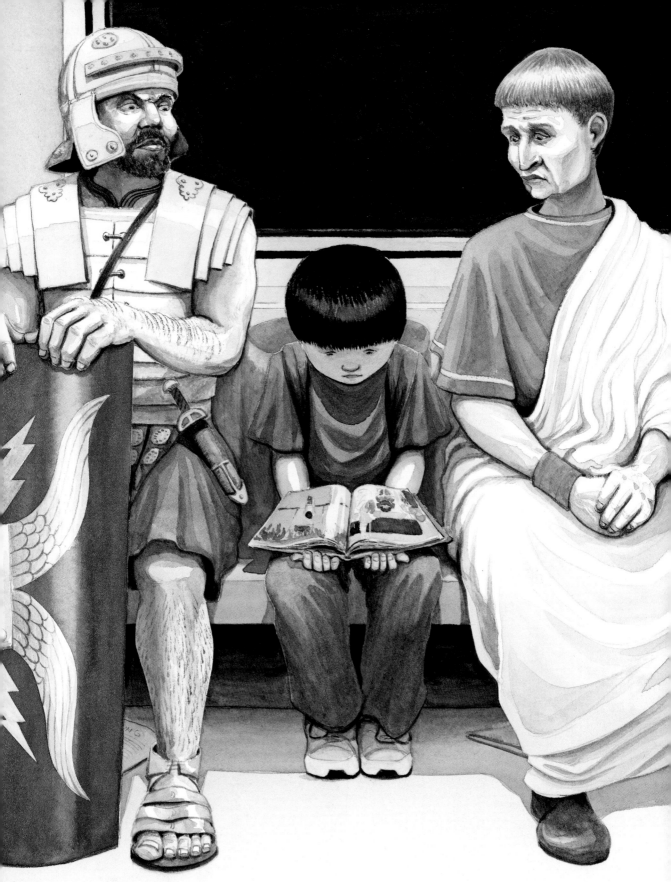

One tree can live for more than 2,000 years,
which means there are trees alive today that
first sprouted during the Roman Empire.

Redwoods have shallow root systems that travel
more than one hundred feet from the tree. They
help the trees stand, and they need all the help
they can get because . . .

they are the tallest living things on the planet. Redwoods regularly grow to be more than 200 feet tall.

A redwood trunk can be
twenty-nine feet in diameter
at its base. That's so wide that a
tunnel can be cut in it, big enough
for a car to drive through.

Amazingly, such a tall tree starts from a seed about the size of a tomato seed. A one-inch-long cone that houses the seed falls to the ground, and if the conditions are right, the tree will sprout. With enough light and water a redwood sapling can grow fast—up to two feet per year.

Redwoods also grow from other redwoods. When a tree falls, or is cut down, new trees can sprout from big round masses along its trunk, called burls. Often several trees will grow from the burls on one stump. If you see a ring of redwoods in the forest, they probably all sprouted from the same stump.

One reason that redwoods are able to live for so long, and grow to be so tall, is that they are very good at defending themselves. Their wood contains a lot of tannin, a chemical that protects them from fungal infections and insect infestations. Redwoods are also well suited to live through fire.

If there is a fire, their extremely thick bark shields them from the heat just like the heat resistant tiles on a space shuttle. Their branches don't start until very high up (200 feet in some cases), which also helps protect them from fire, since most forest fires can't reach their needles.

Even if a fire penetrates a redwood's bark, the tree can
still live. In some cases, a huge portion of the center of
the trunk has been burned out, but the tree keeps on
growing. In many ways, fires actually help redwoods by
clearing out other plants that would otherwise compete
for resources like water and soil.

Coast redwoods need a lot of water to grow as tall as
they do, and the area in Northern California where they
live is perfect—it's a rain forest. The air is cool and
damp, and the land is often covered in thick fog. It takes
a long time for water to travel all the way from the roots
to the top of a redwood, and the fog helps the trees by
preventing them from losing moisture to evaporation.
In addition, the needles of a redwood can absorb
moisture straight from the air.

In the summer, when there is much less rainfall, redwoods have an ingenious way of collecting water: They make their own rain! When the fog rolls in, it condenses on the redwood's needles, and whatever moisture isn't absorbed then falls to the ground to be soaked up by the tree's roots. Other plants that live at the base of a redwood tree use this "artificial rain" as well, so not only do the redwoods water themselves, they water all the plants around them.

The branches of a redwood are called the crown, or canopy, and start very high up the trunk. To study redwood crowns, scientists have to climb into them, and this is not easy. Because the trees are so tall, researchers use a bow and arrow to launch a rope over the branches. When the rope is secure, they can pull themselves up. It is very dangerous work.

When the needles fall off of a redwood, they decay and turn to soil, and redwoods are so big that this soil often collects in the trees themselves. Soil that collects in the branches of a tree, or in crevasses on its trunk, provides a home for other plants. Plants that grow on redwoods are called epiphytes (ep-i-fites). The most common epiphytes found in redwoods are ferns. In one tree, researchers found a mass of ferns weighing more than 1,600 pounds—that's heavier than a full-grown polar bear!

Ferns are not the only plants that make their homes in redwoods. Mosses, fungi, bushes, and even trees grow in the redwood canopy. Researchers have found a wide variety of trees high above the ground, including hemlocks, spruces, firs, oaks, and California bays. In one redwood, researchers found a California bay tree growing out of a knothole over 300 feet from the ground.

In addition to plant life, scientists have found many animals living in the redwood canopy, including flying squirrels, beetles, earthworms, centipedes, spiders, salamanders, and yellow banana slugs. Some animals, like red tree voles, live their whole lives in the treetops and never see the ground.

Many birds live in the tops of redwoods, including bald
eagles, ospreys, and woodpeckers. The marbled murrelet and
the northern spotted owl live almost exclusively in the oldest
redwood trees and are both endangered species.

When a redwood is injured, the tree will often sprout
new trunks that look like miniature versions of the tree
itself. If a branch is damaged, a new trunk will grow
straight up from the top of the damaged branch.
Sometimes more than one new trunk will sprout.
Researchers found one tree with more than 200
reiterated trunks in it—there was a forest of redwoods
growing atop a single tree!

The crown of a redwood can be very complex. As the tree grows, its main branches—and the branches of its new trunks—crisscross and run into each other, forming a maze of growth. The crown can become so dense that from its interior you can't see the ground or the sky. Researchers have even gotten lost while exploring the crown.

The largest of all redwoods are in a class of their own called Titans. For a long time, the record holder for the tallest tree in the world was Stratosphere Giant, measuring a whopping 370 feet.

But that record was broken in the summer of 2006
when researchers discovered Hyperion, a giant coast
redwood rising 379.1 feet from the ground—and it's
still growing.

That's six stories taller
than the Statue of Liberty.

It's taller than
a thirty-story skyscraper.

It's so tall that if it were introduced to
a city skyline, it would fit right in.

REDWOODS IN DANGER

The coast redwood (*Sequoia sempervirens*) used to be found all over North America. After the last ice age, the climate of North America changed, and the habitat conducive to redwood forests shrank. Now they are found only in a small strip of coastland stretching from central California to southern Oregon. In the last 200 years, this forest has shrunk even more because of human activity. Redwood lumber is very valuable because of its height, tannin content, and resistance to harmful bugs such as termites. Since large-scale logging began around 1850, more than 95 percent of the original redwood forests have been destroyed. Only 18 percent of the remaining forests are protected.

When the redwoods go, much of their environment goes too. Many plants depend on them for water in the summer and many animals live nowhere else but in their canopy. Old-growth forests, those forests that have been around for thousands of years and are home to the tallest trees in the world, have ecosystems that are especially fragile. Animals such as the red tree vole, spotted owl, and marbled murrelet only live in old-growth forests. When a forest of this age disappears, it could be another thousand years before it comes back.

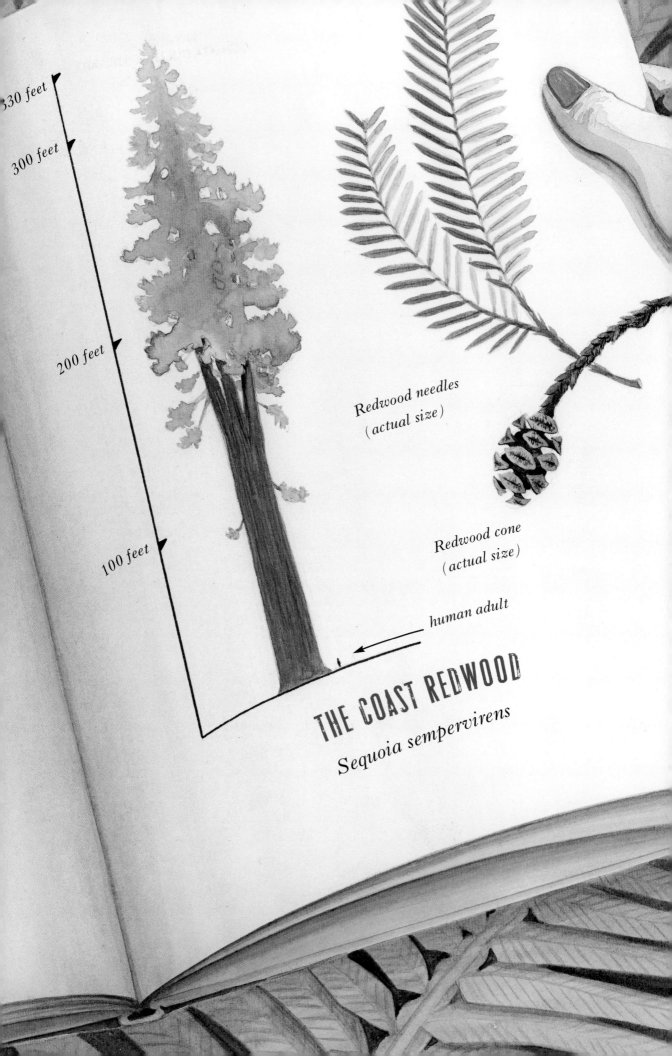

330 feet

300 feet

200 feet

100 feet

Redwood needles
(actual size)

Redwood cone
(actual size)

human adult

THE COAST REDWOOD
Sequoia sempervirens

AUTHOR'S NOTE

I was inspired to create *Redwoods* by the writing
of Richard Preston. I first read his descriptions of
climbing in the redwood canopy in a magazine
article, and then later in his wonderful book, *The
Wild Trees*. After several months of work on this
book, I was fortunate to be able to visit the redwood
forest myself. What I found far exceeded my
expectations, and I left with an affinity for the
redwoods that I hadn't thought possible to have
for a tree. Just as Mr. Preston's writing sparked my
curiosity and awe of these trees, I hope that this
book inspires you. If it does, I hope that you too
can visit California and experience the wonder and
majesty of the redwood forest.